The *One-Minute* Organizer

Plain & Simple

BY DONNA SMALLIN

Storey Publishing

The mission of Storey Publishing is to serve our customers by publishing practical information that encourages personal independence in harmony with the environment.

Edited by Siobhan Dunn
Designed by Wendy Palitz
Cover and interior illustrations © Juliette Borda
Cover photograph by Mark Trembley
Text production by Jennifer Jepson Smith
Indexed by Susan Olason, Indexes & Knowledge Maps

Printed in the United States by CJK
20 19 18 17 16 15 14 13

Library of Congress Cataloging-in-Publication Data

Smallin, Donna, 1960–
    The one-minute organizer plain & simple / Donna Smallin.
        p. cm.
    Includes index.
    ISBN 978-1-58017-584-5 (pbk. : alk. paper)
    1. Home economics. 2. Time management. 3. Storage in the home. I. Title:
    One-minute organizer plain and simple. II. Title.
TX147.S622 2004
640—dc22

2004014567

For every organizer who has gone before me —
and all those who will follow.

Acknowledgments

I believe that our success in this life is largely determined by the company we keep. I want to thank everyone who has helped me along the way, especially the following people:

My colleagues in the National Association of Professional Organizers, for putting the professional in organizing.

Everyone at Storey Publishing who has had a hand in creating and promoting my books, especially Wendy Palitz for the beautiful book covers and layouts; Deborah Balmuth for spearheading this project; Siobhan Dunn for her attention to detail; Sarah Thurston for her enthusiastic publicity efforts; and the entire sales team for doing a bang-up job of getting books into the hands of readers.

My friends and family, for reminding me that it really is a big deal to write a book. Thank you for your love and support.

contents

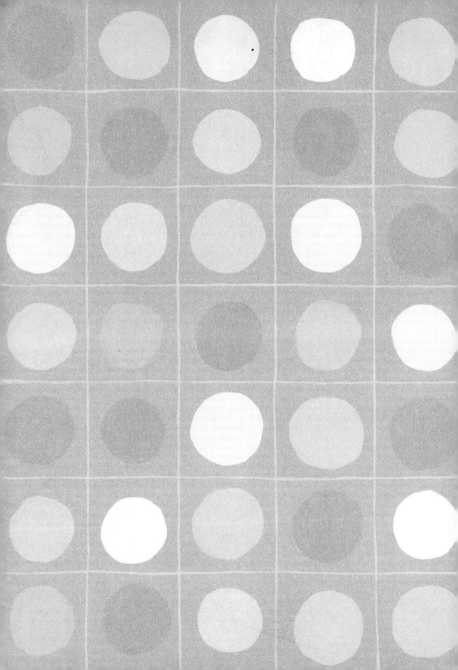

introduction

You struggle to keep up with the chaotic pace of your life. But you keep falling further behind. You want to get organized, but you don't have the time. Or you're so overwhelmed that you don't know where to start.

The reality is that you will never *find* time to get organized. You have to make time, even if it's just five minutes a day. And it doesn't matter *where* you start — only that you get started.

Now is the time. I don't know what makes us think we'll have more time later than we do now. It only looks like that in the present. By the time we get to "later," that imaginary block of free time will have vanished.

Getting Started

You don't have to stop everything to get organized; you just have to start. And you can get started in as little as one minute.

The One-Minute Organizer offers a simple plan to help you unclutter and organize your life . . . one minute at a time. It doesn't promise overnight miracles. It does guarantee success over time by incorporating proven organizing strategies into your daily life.

Start today by making a commitment to spend 5 to 15 minutes a day on one particular area or task. For example, in 15 minutes, you can organize your sock drawer or clear your kitchen counter. In just 10 minutes, you can pare down your shoe collection. In 5 minutes, you can pick up and put away five things.

How to Use This Book

The One-Minute Organizer is the ultimate busy person's guide to getting organized. Every tip in this book can be read in a

matter of seconds; many can be imple-
mented in as little as one minute. Look
for the one-minute symbol -✷- .

You'll find hundreds of simple tips and
ideas to help you tackle every organizing
challenge, including the biggest challenge
— getting your brain in gear. Look to the
orange pages for help with changing some
of the beliefs and behaviors that may have
added to the chaos.

The One-Minute Organizer is divided into
two parts: Getting Organized and Staying
Organized. Chapters are organized by problem areas that represent the most common
organizational challenges. So you can open
to a topic that you find especially trouble-
some and get quick and easy ideas for your
next organizing session. Or turn to the index
to find every tip on a particular subject.

Consistency Is the Key

As you begin to regain control over your physical space, you'll immediately start to feel better and think more clearly. You do realize, of course, that you can't undo years of disorganization in a few days, weeks, or even months. You've got to keep at it.

Strive for consistency. That's the key. Because all of the minutes you spend organizing will eventually add up to a more organized life.

Minutes to a More Organized Life

Daily	Weekly	Monthly
5 minutes	35 minutes	2 hours, 20 minutes
10 minutes	1 hour, 10 minutes	4 hours, 40 minutes
15 minutes	1 hour, 45 minutes	7 hours

PART ONE

Getting Organized

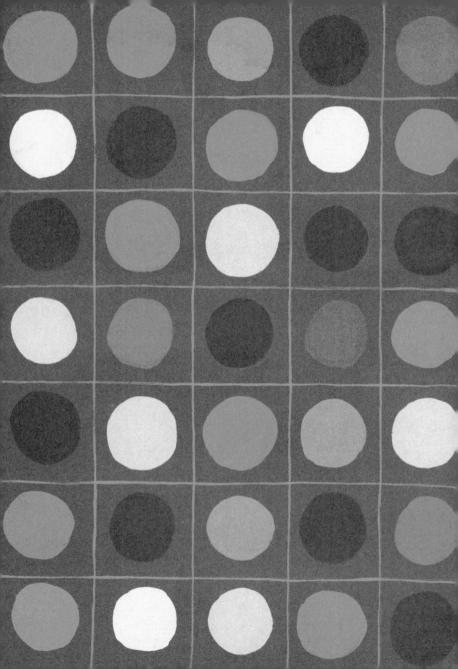

CHAPTER 1

Getting Started

Ninety percent of organizing is getting out of your own way. Think about the beliefs and behaviors that are contributing to the chaos in your life. Before you can change anything, you've got to recognize and accept responsibility for your role and be willing to change the thought patterns and habits that are keeping you from achieving your goal. If you start to think and act like an organized person, you will become one. Fortunately, the more you act the part, the more natural it becomes.

❶ Think about your motivation. What do you stand to gain from getting organized? What do you stand to lose if you don't?

Create a **one-month plan.** Choose five things you most want to organize in the coming month. Number these items from highest to lowest priority. At the end of the month, if you have not yet accomplished all five tasks, create a new one-month plan that outlines what you hope to achieve this month — and what you are willing to do to make it happen.

getting started

Take immediate action. Pick a single organizing tip from this book and **do it today.** Or take 5 minutes right now to organize your sock drawer.

❶ Make today the day you decide to get organized. Tell someone about it.

❶ Start each organizing session this way: Choose a space to organize. Then close your eyes and visualize what that space might look like without clutter and how that would make you feel.

You don't have to stop everything to get organized. You just have to START. Make organizing a part of your daily life. Do it first. Do it fast.

❶ Did you used to be organized? **Think back.** What happened between then and now? Did you move? Start a family or new job? Get married? Divorced? Lose a loved one? Good news: If you were organized at one point in your life, you can get organized again. Believe it!

Start with the most visible clutter first. Seeing clear and obvious results will give you a boost of confidence.

getting started

Talk with your family about why you want to get organized. Ask for their help. You may have to provide some incentive. *Ideas:* Establish a bonus allowance or system of rewards for adhering to new household rules; plan a family night out after a big decluttering project; or agree to put yard sale money toward a family vacation.

Start with **today's mess.** Do whatever it takes to keep up with daily mail, dishes, and laundry. Then set aside time to catch up.

getting started

1 **Commit** to spending a set amount of time every day on un-cluttering and organizing activities. Schedule your organizing sessions for a time when you are mentally fresh. Make an appointment with yourself and write it in your daily planner. Then honor that appointment as you would any other appointment. If you absolutely cannot do this every day, try to schedule in two or three 30-minute sessions each week.

getting started

① Decide in advance what your reward will be for completing each organizing project or room.
Ideas: Plan to buy yourself flowers, treat yourself to a pedicure or massage, or invite friends to enjoy coffee and dessert in your newly uncluttered family room.

Tie your organizing goals into a larger **life goal.** Think about how getting organized will help you to save time or create space so that you can pursue your dreams or simply enjoy a more peaceful life.

Yes, organizing is work.
But there's nothing all
that difficult about it.
The hardest part is
getting STARTED.

getting started

Give yourself a **deadline.** Offer to host a family dinner over the holidays, plan a party at your house, or commit to participating in a neighborhood garage sale.

❶ Establish a daily organizing **reward.** You might, for example, allow yourself to surf the Internet, watch television, or chat on the telephone once your organizing time is up — not before.

❶ Ask a friend to check on your organizing progress one week from today.

getting started

1 Without commitment, nothing gets done. Put your **goal in writing.** Post it on your bathroom mirror or put it in your make-up bag — someplace where it will be a daily reminder.

getting started

● Keep the **end in sight.**
Think about how good you
are going to feel about getting
organized. Try to remember that
feeling whenever you are tempted
to dump a pile of mail on the
kitchen counter or buy one more
thing you really don't need.

● Look at what's working. If you
have been successful in organizing
one particular area, think about
how you can apply that process
elsewhere to create order.

Familiarize yourself with all of the organizing products available. You're apt to find the perfect, ready-made solution for your biggest organizing challenge.

Can't find time to organize? Make time by turning your television on 15 minutes later than usual or turning it off 15 minutes earlier.

Be realistic about what you can and can't do. You can't unclutter your home overnight. You can unclutter a countertop or drawer in as little as 15 minutes.

getting started

Get organized while you watch television. Pull out a **drawer** and dump the contents on the coffee table or floor. During commercials, sort the contents into four piles: throw away, put away (because it belongs in another drawer or somewhere else altogether), give away, and keep. Put back only what you love and/or use.

Start right now. Spend the next 5 minutes picking up **five things** and putting them where they belong.

Get your brain in gear. Complete the following thoughts:

I am disorganized because . . .

The top three things that keep me from getting organized are . . .

What really contributes to the clutter around here is . . .

Clutter makes me feel . . .

I could get more organized if . . .

I want to get organized because . . .

If I could get organized, I could . . .

Our experience is driven by our beliefs. If, for example, you believe that nothing you do makes a difference, that will be your EXPERIENCE. See if you can pinpoint one belief that may be limiting your ability to get organized.

getting started

❶ Set a simple goal. *Example:* "Tonight I'm going to clean out my junk drawer, and then I'm going to stop."

Tackle **one room** at a time. Organize that room one shelf, one drawer at a time.

getting started

1 If you've never been organized it's very likely that you never learned *how* to get organized. You can learn by reading organizing books, attending workshops, and watching how organized people do things. Schedule time to learn organizational skills.

Plan your approach. Random acts of organizing are all well and good, but if you really want to speed up the process, make a plan. Where will you start? How much time will you spend each day?

getting started

Find an **organizing buddy** — someone who wants to get organized as much as you do. Decide to do it together. Make a standing weekly date to show off your accomplishments or discuss progress and share encouragement over the phone.

❶ Ask a friend or family member to help you organize your closet or garage in return for babysitting or help with his or her yard work. Or offer to help with an organizing project.

Organize a progressive **cleaning party.** Invite a few local friends or family members to spend a Saturday at your house, decluttering your basement or garage. Make it fun with food and music. Continue the party next Saturday at the next house.

❶ Consider hiring professional help. Find a local professional organizer through the National Association of Professional Organizers (www.napo.net). A few hours with a professional organizer might be just the jump-start you need.

Keep a **daily journal** of your organizing activities. Take a few minutes each day to jot down how long you spent organizing, what area or things you organized, how you felt afterward, and your goal for tomorrow.

☀ Make organizing time more fun. Turn on the radio or play your favorite CD.

☀ Schedule a personal **victory celebration** for three months from today. Write it in your calendar.

getting started

1 Keep track of your progress. Use a colored marker to mark an X in your **calendar** for each day that you spend at least 5 minutes on uncluttering and organizing activities.

Use the two-pass approach to organizing your entire house. Start by gathering and getting things to the rooms where they belong. In the second pass, you can begin to organize the contents of each room.

What are you doing that contributes to the clutter and chaos in your life? Pick your single worst disorganizing HABIT and work on changing that behavior over the next month.

getting started

Tackle large projects one step at a time. Start by making a list of all of the steps. Then rearrange the steps in order of importance. Working backward from your project deadline, create due dates for each step and incorporate them into your daily calendar. If you don't have a project deadline, create one.

❶ Set a **ticking timer** for the length of your organizing session to help keep you focused on what you are doing.

getting started

❶ Give organizing your full attention. Let your answering machine or voicemail take calls during your organizing sessions.

Did you ever try to get organized but gave up, thinking you were a failure? *You* didn't fail. Your plan failed. Maybe you tried to do too much too fast. Think about what happened and what you learned. **Do it differently** next time, and you will get a different result.

getting started

Make a list of organizing projects, such as filing, photographs, recipes, kitchen, garage. Select one. Break down that project into mini projects. In the kitchen, for example, mini projects might include countertop, under the sink, cutlery drawers, pantry, refrigerator/freezer, recipes, and coupons.

For 5 to 15 minutes each day, work on one **mini project** at a time until the entire organizing project is done. Then check it off your list and move on to the next one.

getting started

Resist the urge to get creative with your organizing systems. It just makes the job harder. Channel your creativity into other areas.

Five ways to motivate a family member to get more organized:

- **Gently communicate what is bothering you and why.**

- **Change the way you are asking (negotiating vs. demanding).**

- **Offer your support in helping to make the change.**

- **Be willing to make compromises.**

- **Be willing to accept that it might not be done exactly as you would do it.**

getting started

1 To make getting organized a priority, tie it to a **financial reward.** What will you do with the money you make selling things you no longer want or need? Use the financial reward as your incentive: The more you get rid of, the more cash you'll have.

Organize your **purse.** Empty it completely. Throw out the trash. Remove items you don't need to carry with you. Make it easier to find things by minimizing the number of units in your purse. Use zippered plastic bags to contain like items, such as lipsticks and other cosmetics.

CHAPTER 2

Clearing Clutter

Unclutter first; then organize. It's so much quicker and easier to get organized when you have less stuff. If you aren't using something and don't have an immediate need for it, it's just taking up valuable space — and making it difficult to find the things you do use and need. Schedule 15 minutes a day to unclutter your space. Even 5 minutes of concentrated effort is better than 0 minutes. Once you get started, you may decide to keep going for the full 15 minutes or longer.

Start with the **easy stuff** — things that don't require any decision making on your part. Grab a trash bag and start tossing in things that are clearly garbage: food wrappers, expired coupons and flyers, stretched-out socks, stained clothing, rusted kitchen utensils, broken items that have since been replaced. Keep going until that trash bag is full.

When uncluttering a shelf, drawer, cupboard, or closet, take everything out. Then put back only those things you love and use.

clearing clutter

- If you are saving something because you *might* need it someday, ask yourself, *"Could I get another one pretty easily and inexpensively if I needed it someday?"* If the answer is yes, **let it go.**

- Can't decide what to keep and what to toss? Ask yourself, *"What's the worst thing that could possibly happen if I decided to let this go?"* If you can live with the consequences, you can live without the thing.

clearing clutter

Pick a room — any room. Now pick **one drawer** or shelf in that room, and start there. Remove everything from a single drawer or shelf and sort stuff into five piles:

1. Throw away
2. Put away
3. Give away
4. Sell
5. Keep

Throw the garbage away. Put away the stuff that belongs elsewhere. Bag or box your donations and anything you plan to sell. Put back only the keepers — those things that you are currently using or absolutely love and can't live without.

☀ **❶** Do you find it difficult to make decisions? Create an **umbrella rule** about when to get rid of things. At what point are you most likely to be willing to part with something you no longer need or use? Six months? One year? Two years? Creating a personal decision-making rule now will eliminate the need to make lots of individual decisions later.

☀ **❶ Be honest** about what you really need to keep.

clearing clutter

1 To keep or toss? Ask yourself:

Have I used this item in the past year?

Will I need it on a definite date in the future?

Do I need to keep it for legal or tax purposes?

Would it be difficult to get another if I needed it again someday?

If you answer no to every question, toss it.

clearing clutter

☀ Still undecided? Ask: *What useful purpose does this thing serve in my life?* If it isn't something you use, is it something that makes you feel good? If not, it's just taking up space. Let it go.

☀ The final step of each clutter-clearing session is the most important: **Schedule your next session.**

clearing clutter

Move out of your living space anything you aren't using but can't bring yourself to let go of. **Box it up.** Write on the box what's inside, and date it. If you haven't needed anything in that box six months or a year from now, donate the whole box.

❶ If you have trouble letting go, think instead in terms of what you want to keep. Make a decision to surround yourself only with **things you love** and use, and remove the rest.

clearing clutter

❶ Recognize that you are not the same person you were 10 years ago. Your **interests, tastes, and styles** have changed. Aim to surround yourself with things that are a part of who you are today. Get rid of anything that is no longer useful or meaningful.

❶ Pretend that you are moving. Ask yourself: *Is this item worth the effort of packing up, carrying out to the moving van, and unpacking at the new place?* If not, give it a new home.

❶ Holding an object increases your attachment to it. Have someone else hold items as you make decisions about what to keep and toss.

❶ A heavy layer of dust on an item is a telltale sign that it's something you don't use. **Give it a new home.**

Too much STUFF?
Getting a bigger house
or apartment is *not*
the solution.

❶ Establish limits on things like plastic **shopping bags** (20 is probably plenty), margarine tubs and yogurt containers (how many do you really need?), rags (only what will fit in a tote bag or bucket), and recycled computer paper (only what fits in a paper tray). Decide in advance what is a reasonable amount to have at any one time. Recycle the excess.

❶ Things have a useful life, and then they become useless. Sure, you can use an old T-shirt as a rag, but do you really need another rag? Give yourself permission to get rid of it.

clearing clutter

☀ Decide to play by the rule: If it's ugly or unfixable, it's out of here.

☀ We often hold on to things we no longer use because we paid "good money" for them. But what is the value of a designer suit that just hangs in your closet, getting older and dustier every year? Zero. **Donate** that suit, and it could be worth $30,000 a year to the woman who wears it to an interview and gets the job.

clearing clutter

① Try to make decisions quickly. If it takes you longer than 60 seconds to decide whether to keep an item, you probably don't really need it.

Once you've made the decision to let go of things, get them out of your home as quickly as possible.

1. Schedule a pickup for your donations, or drive them to the nearest drop-off box.

2. Toss trash the night before your garbage collection day, or take it straight to the dump.

3. Hire a junk removal service.

Aim to surround yourself with BEAUTIFUL and useful things. Give yourself permission to let go of the rest. It's just taking up space and weighing you down.

clearing clutter

If clutter is interfering with your relationships or job, look into joining a **support group.** Check out Messies Anonymous (www.messies.com), Clutterers Anonymous (www.cluttersanony-mous.net), or Clutterless Recovery Groups (www.clutterless.org).

- If it's not your clutter, you are not responsible for it. Give the responsibility — and the stuff — to the rightful owner.

- Do not save things to sell at a garage or yard sale unless you have set a definite date for that sale. Donate those items instead.

❶ Recognize that your time is valuable. It takes a lot of time and energy to plan and hold a successful **garage sale.** You may be better off taking the tax deduction if you itemize on your tax return. If you make a donation valued at $400, you will save a percentage in taxes equal to your highest ending tax bracket. Do the math.

Create a list of your tax-deductible donations, and assign values to each. Check out the valuation guide at www.salvationarmyusa.org.

clearing clutter

Look for a **local charity** that accepts donations of everything from books to clothing to household furnishings. *Better:* Find one that will send a truck to pick up your donations.

☀ Schedule a pickup with a local charity to come and get your donations one week from today, or make a note in your calendar to drive your donations to their destination.

☀ When making decisions about **sentimental items,** decide to keep only those things that hold happy memories.

Some PROGRESS is

better than no progress.

Don't waste time trying to sell junk. Trash stuff that's become outdated or obsolete, such as college textbooks, old computer equipment, and anything that's unfixable. No one wants it — not even as a donation.

① Weigh the pain of letting go of stuff you aren't using against the pain of living with it all. Sure, there's a slight chance that you might miss something after it's gone. But 99 percent of the time, you'll never think of it again. **Have faith** that you will make the right decision!

clearing clutter

☀ Don't think of uncluttering as getting rid of stuff. Think of it as giving to someone who needs it more than you, or as **recycling.**

☀ If something holds a great deal of sentimental value and you absolutely cannot part with it, don't!

clearing clutter

Take photos of your child with favorite artwork or school projects. Put the photos in your photo album and let go of the physical items.

❶ Take a photograph of sentimental items before parting with them.

If you have clutter, you are richer than you think. Look at uncluttering as an opportunity to SHARE your abundance — the stuff you don't need — with people who could really use it.

clearing clutter

☀ Accept that you can't control life by holding on to things. The secret is to let go.

☀ Decide to have a "giving away" party for **inherited** estate items. Invite family and friends to tag items they would like to take. Donate any untagged items after the party.

What's the point of keeping **memorabilia** in storage? No one can enjoy it there. Look for ways to display, and even use, cherished items.

clearing clutter

Instead of saving everything that once belonged to a loved one, find a way to **honor the memories** attached to various things. *Idea:* Videotape a family gathering where family members are invited to share their remembrances about particular items. Then donate or give the items away. Or sell valuables and make a donation in the deceased's name.

Create a **keepsake box** for saving love letters, cards, artwork, and other memorabilia. If you have little storage space, limit boxes to one per household member.

clearing clutter

☀ If you are afraid to let go of something, do it scared. The act of letting go of material possessions can also help you let go of guilt, grudges, and other **emotional garbage.**

Turn clutter into cash by:

- **Having a garage or yard sale.**

- **Advertising big-ticket items.**

- **Selling items on consignment.**

- **Selling to a secondhand store.**

- **Selling online.**

clearing clutter

Unclutter your **work space.**
Create a main storage area for office
supplies — in a drawer, cabinet, or
closet. Put like items together.
Doing so will make it easy to see
what you have and what you need.

Clear your **desktop,** and put
back only what you use daily.
Store everything else in drawers,
on shelves, or in your supply closet.

clearing clutter

Set up **clutter collectors** where clutter naturally tends to collect: a bowl on the counter for keys and loose change, a set of tiered baskets for collecting mail and school paperwork, a coat tree or wall hooks in the entryway for hanging outerwear and backpacks.

Unclutter your walls. Take down everything, and put back only what you love. Group framed photographs together in one space, for a more dramatic, less cluttered look. If you have too many **wall hangings** to display at one time, put some into storage and rotate them when the seasons change.

clearing clutter

Get rid of bath and shower items you haven't used in more than a month. Move extras into a guest bathroom, or pour them into travel-size containers. Donate the rest.

Clear **bathroom** countertops. Put back the soap and anything else that absolutely must remain out. Store everything else in cabinets and drawers. Use handled baskets or bags for easy storage and removal of daily toiletries.

clearing clutter

Clean out your **medicine cabinet.** Throw away leftover doses of medicines, expired prescriptions, and over-the-counter products.

Toss makeup products you never wear.

Check expiration dates and toss:

- **Perfume more than three years old.**

- **Makeup more than one year old.**

- **Sunscreen more than two years old.**

- **Anything past its expiration date.**

clearing clutter

Use caution when disposing of unused medicines and vitamins. Flush pills and liquids down the toilet; put all other items into a lidded coffee can or plastic bag secured with a twist tie, and dispose of them in a lidded trash can that children, pets, and wildlife cannot get into.

Clear out enough space on shelves and in cabinets and closets to make it easy to see what you've got and to **allow room** for future storage.

Clear **kitchen** countertops, and put back only what you use at least twice a week. Store everything else in cabinets and drawers.

❶ Designate certain shelves or areas of your refrigerator for storing **leftovers.** It will increase the likelihood that the leftovers won't be forgotten.

❶ Label and date all leftover containers. Keep labels and markers handy.

clearing clutter

Add a carousel tray to one or more shelves in your **refrigerator** to enable easy access to items in the back. Or corral like items, such as snacks or condiment jars, in a large plastic container that you can pull forward as needed.

Schedule some time to play "dress-up" in your **closet.** Try on everything. If it fits and you love it, hang it back up.

Separate castoffs into categories: donations, repairs and alterations, consignment/yard sale.

❶ Move special-occasion **clothes** and **accessories** to one end of your closet to make it easier to get to everyday clothes.

clearing clutter

Starting at one end of your closet, work your way across and remove any items you haven't worn in the last year. If you haven't worn them in the past year, you are not likely to wear them in the coming year. Donate them now rather than later, and enjoy the **extra space** in your closet.

Keep in your everyday closet and drawers only those clothes that fit you. Remove anything you don't wear because it doesn't look or feel good on you.

clearing clutter

☀ If you can't bring yourself to let go of clothes you are not wearing, decide to put them with your out-of-season clothes. You may be ready to donate them six months or a year from now when you see them again.

☀ Toss promotional items and other freebies you are not using.

clearing clutter

As you unclutter closets and drawers, make **three piles:** A, B, and C. The A pile is for clothes you wear and like and definitely want to keep. The B pile is a "maybe" pile. The C pile is for things you haven't worn in ages. Put the A pile away. Then go though the B pile again. Donate clothes in the C pile.

CHAPTER 3

Paper Stuff

Paper is a daily part of modern life. But left unchecked, it can quickly grow into a bigger part than we would like! The secret to minimizing pileup is to establish a plan for dealing with each category of paper — everything from newspapers, catalogs, and magazines to mail, notes, lists, and receipts. It means making decisions. What do you really need to save? How and where should it be filed? Start by organizing your most important day-to-day papers first. Then tackle the less urgent papers.

paper stuff

Start by making a **first pass.** Gather in one place all the piles of papers that are strewn throughout your home or office. Do a quick sort of papers. Put into boxes everything except your most important papers — generally project-related, financial, or papers with a deadline. In the second pass, you can begin to begin to make decisions about each piece of paper. Meanwhile, you know where all your unfiled papers are.

paper stuff

Turn piles into files. First step: Take a sample pile and make a list of the types of papers you find. This will help you figure out what type of files you may need to create.

Sort day-to-day papers into **action files:** bills to pay, receipts to enter, papers to photocopy, data for reports, items to file or discuss with your boss or spouse, or papers to forward to another department or family member. Create labeled folders for these action files, and store them upright in a stepped desktop organizer.

paper stuff

Establish a home for unpaid bills.
Ideas: Create an action file for
your desktop or a folder for a
filing cabinet drawer. Or file all
bills and receipts in an expandable
file with pockets for each month
so you can pay bills and do your
filing anywhere.

Make it easier to **pay bills.**
Keep handy a supply of envelopes,
return-address labels, stamps,
pens, a calculator, and a stapler.

paper stuff

A **simple system** for bi-monthly bill payment: File bills that need to be paid in the second half of the month in a folder labeled "Due 16–31," and file those that need to be paid between the 1st and 15th in a file labeled "Due 1–15." Put both files in a hanging folder labeled "Bills Due." Or file the two categories in a two-pocket folder. Make a note in your calendar to pay bills on the dates you choose as your bill-paying dates.

paper stuff

Sort before filing. Use hanging files in an empty cardboard file storage box or a rolling file cart to sort papers into **filing categories** such as insurance, taxes, and receipts. Attach a sticky note to the top of each hanging folder to identify the category — these are your sorting folders. Once you've sorted all your papers, transfer the papers from each category into an existing folder in your filing cabinet or, if necessary, add a file tab to your sorting folder and file the folder and all. The beauty of this sorting system is that you can do your sorting in front of the television or wherever it is comfortable.

paper stuff

1 Remember that the reason you file something is so that you can retrieve it. When naming a new file, think of what heading you are likely to look under should you need that document. Don't think too long about this; the first name that springs to mind is probably the best file name.

1 Do not store **your will** in a safe-deposit box rented in your name only. The box will be sealed on your death, which could delay the transfer of your assets. Make a photocopy for your home files, and have your attorney keep the original.

paper stuff

➊ Avoid labeling files and folders as **"Miscellaneous."** If the information isn't important enough to have its own label, it either belongs in another folder or it's not important enough to save.

Align hanging-file tabs in the same position on every hanging folder. It makes it easier to see the labels when they're all in a line. Plus you can add and subtract folders from the drawer without messing up a zigzag pattern.

paper stuff

Refer to the following standard home filing categories as a guide to setting up your own:

- Insurance — auto, home, life, disability, medical

- Financial — bank accounts, credit accounts, mortgage statements, investments

- Property — receipts for home improvements, furnishings and valuables, product manuals and receipts, automotive purchases and repair receipts

- Taxes — current-year receipts and other tax documentation

- Medical records

- Veterinary records

paper stuff

❶ If the stack of paper in a file folder is more than one inch thick, separate the stack into two folders.

❶ Choose staples over paper clips for keeping papers together in a file. Paper clips tend to fall off or get attached to unrelated papers.

paper stuff

① Insert hanging-file tabs on the front of the folder so that they're visible even when the folder is full. When you want to look in the folder, just pull the tab forward to open the file in the drawer.

Color-code hanging file tabs to distinguish between different types of files such as financial or insurance records. Also use **color coding** to separate business and personal files or to differentiate project or client folders.

Information gets OUTDATED quickly. If you know where to find the most current information, there's no need to file the paper.

paper stuff

Don't waste time filing papers you don't need to save. For example, there is no legal or tax reason to save your cable bill and other utility bills after paying them unless needed to **document** business expenses. You may wish to keep just the most current paid bill as documentation that your last payment was received or for easy reference to customer service numbers. Shred the rest.

paper stuff

❶ If you like to compare utility usage from month to month, simply note amounts on a single sheet of paper or spreadsheet.

❶ It's a smart practice to save product purchase **receipts** for 30 to 90 days in case you decide to return an item. Create a folder labeled "Current Receipts." File the newest receipts up front. Periodically shred older receipts.

paper stuff

To document value for property insurance claims, create an itemized list of high-value items such as jewelry, furniture, and artwork. Store receipts in a **safe-deposit box.**

❶ Keep credit card receipts until you receive your credit card statement and verify each purchase. Then shred them unless (a) you need the receipts to document business expenses or (b) you want to document your purchase for warranty or other purposes.

paper stuff

Create hanging file folders for all **owner's manuals,** or store them in one or more three-ring binders with three-hole punched clear plastic pockets. Organize them alphabetically by category — for example, television or refrigerator — or by the room in which the product resides.

☀ Staple product receipts to owner's manuals.

☀ Shred receipts for items you no longer own.

If you had 20 minutes to evacuate your home and could take only what you could fit in your car, what would you take? Most things can be easily replaced. Once you realize this, it's easier to LIGHTEN your load.

paper stuff

Once reviewed and paid, **credit card** statements don't need to be saved except to document business expenses for tax purposes. If you feel more comfortable saving them, limit yourself to 12 consecutive monthly statements.

❶ Keep only the current billing statement for property and automotive **insurance policies.** Discard the previous year's statement and documentation when you receive the new policy information.

paper stuff

When your annual **investment** statement arrives, shred the quarterly statements. Keep only the most current year's prospectus and addenda.

Free up space in your filing cabinets by eliminating papers and files you no longer need. Start in one drawer, and work from front to back. Mark where you left off so you know where to begin again.

paper stuff

Try a numerical system for "idea" files. Label a hanging folder "ideas." Label a manilla folder "1". Write "1" in the upper right-hand corner of the first 10–12 "idea" papers and put them in the manilla folder. On your computer, create a master index with two to five keywords to describe each paper. Create and number as many folders as you need to file all your papers. To retrieve a particular document, use the keyword search feature in your word processing program.

paper stuff

❶ Shred all **financial documents** and any paper with personally identifiable information, including prescription labels, to minimize the possibility of identity theft or fraud.

For complete and current guidelines for keeping tax-related paperwork, refer to IRS Publication 552, "Recordkeeping for Individuals" at www.irs.gov/pub/ or ask your tax adviser.

Don't worry about coming up with the PERFECT organizing system for bills or filing. Done is perfect.

paper stuff

Set up a tax file. File all tax documentation immediately. Create labeled file folders for the following:

- **Income — Pay stubs, W-2s, 1099s, interest and dividend statements**

- **Donations — Receipts for charitable donations (cash and noncash)**

- **Medical — Receipts for medical expenses**

- **Real estate — Mortgage interest statements, real estate tax statements**

- **Child care — Receipts for child care payments**

Also file any correspondence you receive from the Internal Revenue Service or state revenue department.

paper stuff

① Studies show that 80 percent of what gets filed never gets looked at again. Before filing a piece of paper, question whether you really need to. *Do you need it for legal or tax reasons?* Save it. Is there a copy filed somewhere else? Toss it.

Store inactive files away from active files. You might think you need to buy more filing cabinets when all you really need to do is free up space by **archiving** inactive files. Tax files and completed project folders are good examples.

paper stuff

Remove archived files — hanging folder and all — to an upper shelf of a closet or in your attic, dry basement, or garage. It's helpful to **store** these files in same-size boxes that can be neatly stacked. Look for sturdy white cardboard file boxes with lids that you can buy in any office-supply store. These boxes are designed with a rim around the inside for storing hanging folders. Label the front of each box — for example, "TAX RETURNS 1990–1999."

paper stuff

Rent a safe-deposit box to store important financial and legal documents and any other items that would be difficult or impossible to replace, including:

- Marriage, birth, death certificates

- Settlement and divorce papers

- Adoption, custody, citizenship, military papers

- Trust papers, living will, powers of attorney

- Property deeds, motor vehicle titles

- Stock and bond certificates

- U.S. Savings Bonds

- All contracts

- Home inventory list, photos, receipts for valuables

paper stuff

☀ Rather than save entire magazines for future reference **tear out** and file only the articles.

☀ Put magazines and other reading material where you are most likely to read it — in your briefcase for the commute home, for example, or on your nightstand.

paper stuff

Binders are a simple, convenient way to store reference material. To decide between binder and file storage, ask yourself:

Would it be helpful if this information were portable?

Do I need to cross-reference information?

Do I have convenient shelf space for binder storage?

If the answer to all three questions is no, a filing drawer may be a better solution.

paper stuff

Use binders to file newspaper and magazine **clippings.** Create one binder for each main category, such as "Home Decorating Ideas" or "Vacation Ideas." Insert articles in top-loading clear plastic sheet protectors. Use tabbed index sheets to create sections — for example, "Bathroom," "Bedroom," "Kitchen."

paper stuff

1 If you're a little behind on your reading material, schedule reading time into every day so you can catch up.

1 If you're way behind on your reading, scan the table of contents of each magazine. **Highlight** only the most interesting articles, and read just those before recycling the magazine.

1 Get caught up on your reading in less than 60 seconds. Toss everything in your **"to read" pile,** and vow to keep up from this point forward.

Next time you hear yourself complaining about not having TIME to get organized, stop. All we have is time. How we choose to use it is up to us.

paper stuff

Consider canceling subscriptions to **magazines** you haven't read in the past three months. You will likely receive a refund for the unused portion of your subscription. You may also have the option to temporarily suspend your subscription. Or you can donate the remainder of your subscription to a friend or family member by requesting to change the mailing name and address.

paper stuff

① **Put a limit** on the number of magazines you subscribe to, which might be half the number you receive now. If you miss any of them, you can always buy an issue or resubscribe at a later date.

① Don't keep every issue of every magazine. **Decide** now how many of each you would like to keep or have room to store. Recycle the rest.

paper stuff

☀ ❶ If you have piles of **unopened mail** offers, dump them in your recycling or trash bin. Don't even give it a second thought, because more of the same are already on the way.

☀ ❶ Save only the newest versions of **catalogs.** Toss those you rarely or never order from.

Let go of beliefs such as:

- It's just going to get messed up again.

- I don't know where to start.

- I don't have time.

- I don't know how.

- I've tried to get organized before and failed.

paper stuff

Reduce the amount of **unsolicited mail** you receive. Send a postcard or letter to the Direct Marketing Association, Mail Preference Service, P.O. Box 643, Carmel, NY 10512. Ask to have your name and address removed from all of their mailing lists. Allow several months for the deluge to subside.

❶ Here's a nifty trick for storing professional or office supply catalogs in a filing cabinet: Open the catalog to roughly the center and then hang it over the top edges of a hanging file.

paper stuff

❶ Designate a basket or paper tray where children can put all **school papers** that require your attention: permission slips, graded homework and tests, and notices.

Set up a system for returning paper-work to children. *Ideas:* Create a folder for each child to check each morning or hand out paperwork at the breakfast table.

Use large magnetic refrigerator clips to organize upcoming **event flyers** in date order, collect take-out menus, or post schedules for team practices and games.

paper stuff

Cardboard dressers are a simple, inexpensive solution for storing school papers, artwork, and mementos. Give each child a dresser or assign drawers to children in a shared room.

School-age children will benefit from having their own filing cabinet or drawer. **Teach children** how to set up hanging file folders for each subject and how to file and purge papers at the end of the year to make room for next year's papers.

Recognize that it's natural to feel some fear about getting organized even when the change is desired. Getting organized one minute at a time ALLOWS you to make a gradual adjustment from familiar territory into new territory.

paper stuff

Organize **recipes** in a three-ring binder. Use tabbed index sheets to create sections — for example, "Appetizers," "Desserts," and "Untried Recipes." Sort recipes by category. Then insert same-category recipes back-to-back in top-loading clear plastic sheet protectors. Affix odd-size clippings, notes, or recipes to a sheet of 8½-x-11-inch paper for easier insertion.

paper stuff

Determine whether the savings you get from **coupons** are worth the time it takes to clip, file, and retrieve them. If you decide to continue using coupons, toss all expired coupons. If you haven't used grocery coupons in the past three months, toss them all.

Store coupons in a mini expandable file with dividers for food categories or your store's aisle numbers.

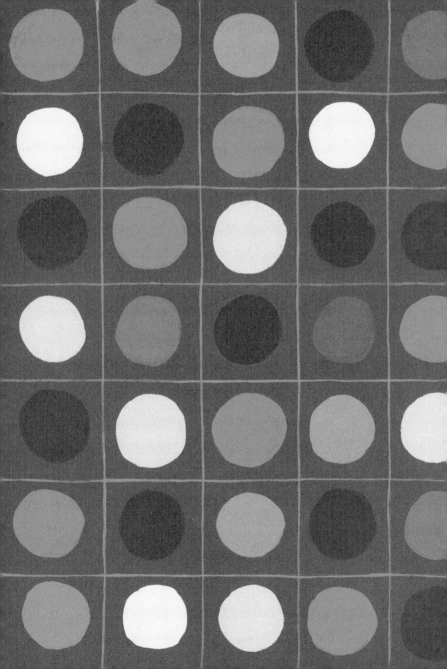

CHAPTER 4

Spaces & Things

Find a home for every homeless thing. Look at the stuff that never gets put away. Chances are it has nowhere to go. Organizing is about finding a place for everything so you can always put everything in its place — and put your hands on it when you need it. A good place for a particular item is one that is convenient to where the item is used. Once you decide on a home for something, you never have to think again about what to do with it. Just put it in its place.

Organize one room at a time.

☀ Question the placement of everything. Ask: *Why is this here? Is there a better place for it?*

☀ To decide what goes where in any space, use the **"HOT/WARM/ COLD" rule.** If it's used frequently (HOT), keep it handy. If it's used occasionally (WARM), you can get up and walk to it. If it's rarely used (COLD), you can climb for it.

Arrange the contents of cabinets and closets so that **frequently used items** are the most accessible. Store less frequently used items on very high or low shelves in a closet or at the back of a cabinet.

Store items used most frequently at about waist height. If you have to choose between higher and lower, choose higher.

Move anything you are not using out of your everyday living/working space.

spaces & things

Set up **workstations** for activities such as handling mail and bills, sewing, hobbies, and laundry. Organize your workstation with all the supplies you need.

☀ ❶ Put scissors, tape, pens, paper, and other tools in places where you commonly use them.

spaces & things

Pay attention to the areas that frustrate you. Could better organization diffuse your frustration? Make a note to organize that area in your next organizing session. Or take a 15-minute time-out and get a start right now.

Walk through your home. Look for ways to use doors, walls, and even ceilings as **vertical storage** space: back-of-door organizers, shelving, hooks, Peg-Boards, racks, and grid systems.

Look for and use **hidden storage** spaces:

- Store wrapping paper and supplies in an under-the-bed box. Or stand paper rolls in the corner of a closet; hang ribbon and bows in a plastic bag clipped to a hanger with a clothespin.

- Keep remote controls and small "cluttery" items in a decorative basket or tin on a shelf where you will see only the container.

- When buying furniture, choose items that double as storage spaces: trunk-style coffee tables, beds with drawers, and covered benches.

People have power over things — not the other way around. Vow to use that power to REGAIN CONTROL of your space and time.

spaces & things

Label everything: folders, home videos, boxes, bins, binders, shelves. Use a marker or a label maker to create neatly lettered, easy-to-read labels.

1 When looking for more storage space, don't forget to look up. Sometimes the best solution is to hang items.

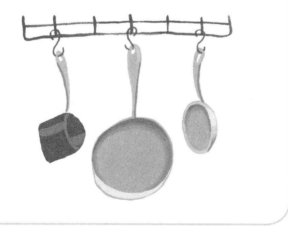

Collect all clothing with missing buttons, fallen hems, or rips and put it in a bag for **mending.** Schedule mending time, or take those items to a seamstress or tailor.

Need to frame a picture, repair your favorite pair of shoes, or get a new battery for your watch? Put these items in the trunk of your car, and schedule a time to take them where they need to go.

❶ Designate a place near the door you use most often, where you can put **videos** or library books that need to be returned, outgoing mail, and items to go to the dry cleaner.

1 Keep a small spiral notebook handy during organizing sessions. **Jot down** any organizing projects that should be dealt with in a separate session. Making a note will help to keep you from getting sidetracked.

1 Place a basket or a shoe rack near the front door to collect shoes.

1 Use a decorative **screen** to hide a shoe bin in the entryway, to partition off a workstation, or to keep archived storage boxes out of sight.

No office? File household papers in a rolling file drawer. Store it in a closet, and take it out as needed.

No coat closet? Install **pegs** along one wall, or get a coatrack for collecting backpacks, jackets, and hats that would otherwise end up where they don't belong. Be sure to hang hooks for children at an appropriate height.

Use adjustable dividers, drawer organizers, small boxes or trays, or even zippered plastic storage bags to organize similar things.

spaces & things

Arrange **books** the way they are organized in bookstores and libraries. Separate fiction from nonfiction. *One step further:* Organize fiction alphabetically by author. Organize nonfiction by type — biographies, history, and travel, for example — and then alphabetically by author.

Group collectibles together in one display for a less cluttered look.

On the back of any door hang a **shoe bag** with clear plastic pockets to create instant, convenient storage for magazines, cleaning supplies, small toys, pantry items, craft items, or hand tools.

Store out-of-season blankets, comforters, coats, sweaters, and other **seasonal** clothing in vacuum-compressed bags to save space.

spaces & things

Use empty **suitcases** to store out-of-season clothing or bedding in a closet or under a bed. Use locking suitcases to store things you don't want the children to find.

❶ Store an extra set of sheets between the mattress and box spring at the foot of the bed.

Clear **plastic storage bins** with lids are the organizer's favorite product. Figure out how many you need. Buy same-size boxes for neat and easy stacking.

Copy-paper boxes are the next best thing to plastic storage bins. They're lidded, sturdy, stackable, and free. Bring some home from work and use them to store holiday decorations, memorabilia, hand-me-down toys, or out-of-season shoes and accessories. Or use them to store and carry donation items.

❶ Clearly label the front of each storage box.

There's a difference between being organized and being NEAT and tidy. Stashing stuff in drawers and putting folders and papers in tidy stacks isn't necessarily organized. Always choose "organized" over "neat."

spaces & things

❶ Store boxes and bins with labels facing out so you can find what you're looking for without having to move heavy boxes.

Consider numbering each box and keeping on your computer a **master index** that includes the box number, list of contents, and location of the box. If you need to retrieve an item, use the "find" feature in your word processing program and a keyword to locate items or tape to the box an itemized list of the contents; you'll be able to find a particular item without having to open boxes.

spaces & things

1 Designate a storage zone in your basement or garage where you can keep all storage items.

Use open **plastic crates** on shelves for categorizing and storing items that require easy access, such as camping, biking, or skiing equipment or lawn games.

1 Keep an open catchall box in your storage area to collect items that need to be added to packed boxes. Put **catchall items** where they belong the next time you pull out the boxes.

In your garage, basement, or shed, create storage between exposed studs. Nail two-by-fours at one-foot intervals to create vertical bins for long-handled lawn and garden tools and sports equipment.

Recycle lidded glass jars and coffee cans into containers for sorting, separating, and storing **hardware** in the workshop.

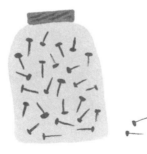

spaces & things

❶ Decide to use off-site storage as a last resort.

If you are currently renting storage space, schedule a visit to your storage unit. Evaluate: *Is it really worth the money to store this stuff, or could you get rid of some or most or even all of it?*

If you begin to doubt your ABILITY to organize, remember this: You can do anything you set your mind to do.

spaces & things

Arrange your **office** so that you can reach your telephone, keyboard, printer, and wastebasket without getting up.

Be sure to distribute weight in vertical filing cabinets; opening a full top drawer with empty or partly filled bottom drawers can cause the cabinet to tip over.

Organize your **desk drawers** so that each contains like items — for example, office supplies in one drawer, stationery and notepads in another.

Solve the problem of what to do with bathrobes and wet towels with an over-the-door peg rack.

If bathroom storage space is minimal, give each family member a portable **shower caddy** for transporting toiletries from bedroom to bathroom and back.

Make more room for everyday bathroom items by storing first aid supplies, over-the-counter remedies, and vitamins in the guest room bathroom or in a kitchen cabinet.

Store **kitchen items** where you use them: pots and pans near the stove, food-storage wraps and containers near the refrigerator, dishes and silverware near the dishwasher or table.

Store items in a way that makes sense to you. You might, for example, store coffee filters, the sugar bowl, and coffee spoons with your coffee cups or store measuring cups and spoons in a large mixing bowl.

Pull out large and seldom-used kitchen items — the turkey roasting pan, clam steamer, and punch bowl — and store in a more out-of-the-way area, such as a hall closet shelf, the garage, or the basement.

Don't store frequently used items in cabinets above the **stove;** if you reach for them while cooking you could burn yourself.

spaces & things

Organize a messy cabinet or pantry by making use of empty vertical space. Use double-decker turntables, sliding baskets, hanging shelves, stackable containers, and other inexpensive organizing products, including cup hooks.

In the **kitchen pantry,** organize shelves and areas by type of food such as pastas, cereals, and soups. Categorizing makes it quicker and easier to find a particular item. Labeling shelves enables anyone to help put away groceries.

1 The average woman has 40 pairs of **shoes.** The average man has 10. Count yours.

If you have an above-average number of shoes, pull out those you no longer wear, and donate them. Somebody somewhere could really use them.

Separate shoes into regular wear and occasional wear. Keep those you wear regularly visible and accessible on a **shoe rack** or in clear plastic shoe boxes, stacked on shelves. Store special-occasion shoes on upper shelves, in a corner, or against a back wall.

If you store shoes in their original boxes, take an instant photograph of each pair of shoes and glue it to the front of the box to identify what's inside.

Trying to organize your entire home IN A DAY is like trying to eat an entire piece of cake in one bite. You'd choke. Work on organizing projects in small chunks.

Try storing **panty hose** and socks in a hanging shoe bag with clear plastic pouches. Organize by color and type, such as knee-highs, dress sheers, and sports socks. The best part about this organizing trick is that you don't even have to fold them when you put them away. Just stuff them in the pockets.

Hang like items together in your closet. **Sort clothing** in categories such as special occasion, business, and casual. Further sort into subcategories, such as pants, skirts, and long- and short-sleeved shirts. Or organize by color.

spaces & things

Double **closet space** for shorter items by attaching a hanging clothes rod to your existing rod.

☀ Set a goal to keep things off the floor of your closet. It's less cluttered and makes it easier to vacuum.

If your dresser drawers are over-stuffed and you have room in your closet, consider getting a hanging **garment bag** with shelves. It will give you easy access to bulky sweaters, T-shirts, and jeans.

Organize your dresser one drawer at a time. Organize your closet in sections. Otherwise you may create a bigger mess than you started with.

Screw hooks in your bedroom closets to **hang robes,** pajamas, and other clothing that will be reworn. Add one hook where you can hang the entire outfit you plan to wear the next day.

❶ Hang a nylon or mesh bag on a hook in your closet to collect items that need to go to the dry cleaner.

Organize **jewelry** in ice cube trays. Store one set of earrings or one fine chain necklace in each cube. Stack in a drawer.

❶ Place a pretty dish on dresser tops and nightstands to collect jewelry, loose change, and pocket paraphernalia.

String a nylon hammock across a **child's room** to store stuffed animals or in a corner of the garage to create a home for balls, gloves, helmets, knee pads, and other sports gear.

Organize and store toys in colorful plastic dishpans on shelves. **Toy boxes** tend to create clutter, because kids have to take out everything to find the one thing they want.

In a young child's closet, install a tension rod at a reachable height and raise it as the child grows.

spaces & things

❶ Make it easy and fun for kids to put things away, and they will be more likely to maintain a clutter-free room. *Example:* Place a basket or crate on the closet floor to throw shoes into.

Stack plastic crates in a child's closet for storing folded sweaters, T-shirts, and jeans.

Colorful interlocking plastic crates make great **cubbyholes** for storing books, toys, and games.

Organize toys in see-through plastic bins by themes. *Examples:* building blocks, cars, animals.

Bed elevators are a great way to create instant under-the-bed storage space for toys or seasonal bedding and clothes. Some lift the bed high enough to create a little play area or room for a desk.

spaces & things

On a **tight budget?** Try these no-cost ideas:

1. Ask for a clean large pizza box to use as a child's artwork portfolio that can be stored under a bed.

- Use children's artwork to decorate their rooms. Replace older artwork periodically with newer artwork.

1. Give kids shoeboxes for storing their tiniest collectibles.

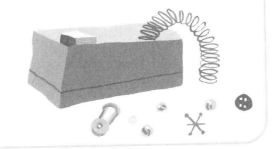

spaces & things

1 Schedule a regular time each week to sort and organize photographs until you are up-to-date. Wait to buy **photo albums** or photo boxes until you know how many you need.

Divide **photographs** into five to seven broad categories, such as "Friends," "Family," "Grandchildren," "Places We've Lived," and "Places We've Visited." Or categorize by events (graduations), time frames (college days), or family members. Sort photographs by category into labeled shoe boxes or photo boxes.

spaces & things

Sort one category of photographs into subcategories. For example, if the category is vacations, sort photographs into separate vacations you've taken.

Use labeled paper grocery bags cut down to about six inches high as temporary holders for organizing subcategories of photographs.
Or use an **accordion file** with labeled folders.

spaces & things

❶ Select your preferred photo-storage medium and stick with it: photo albums or archival photo boxes with dividers.

❶ Throw away photographs that didn't come out right or are very similar to other, better photographs.

❶ Throw out duplicate photographs, or put them in an envelope marked **"Duplicates"** and store at the back of the album or box that holds the originals.

PART TWO

Staying Organized

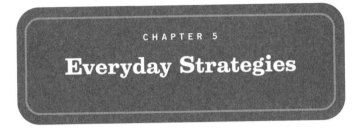

CHAPTER 5

Everyday Strategies

It's a lot easier to keep up than to catch up. So start by organizing the everyday stuff. Set up systems to help you stay on top of appointments, pay bills, and manage information. Don't worry about setting up the perfect system. You can always perfect it later. Do be on the lookout for ways to simplify everyday tasks. Take note of the tasks you tend to avoid doing. Organizing these areas will make it simpler to complete these tasks and also bring you the greatest reward.

If you're feeling a little stressed, it may be that things are getting out of control. **Regain control** by taking time out to organize something. You'll feel better immediately.

1 Before you set something down, ask yourself, *"Is this where it belongs?"* If not, take an extra minute or two to put it in its place.

1 Create a home for new acquisitions right away.

Get into "wash and wear."
Look for and buy clothes that
are machine washable and don't
need to be ironed.

Use the time it takes to brew a
pot of coffee to organize a cutlery
drawer, remove out-of-date food
from the refrigerator, or write a
grocery list.

Limit the number of **daily decisions** you have to make. *Examples*: Plan weekly meals in advance and post the plan on the refrigerator. Pare down your wardrobe to your favorite outfits to make it easier to decide what to wear.

❶ Jot all notes, reminders, and phone numbers in a small spiral notebook. It eliminates all the little bits of paper and sticky notes that are apt to get lost. And if you need to retrieve a piece of information, you know where it is.

Get your **hair** styled in a way that is natural so you don't have to spend so much time fussing with it.

❶ Unclutter your **mind.** Get in the habit of writing things down rather than trying to remember them.

① Want to **keep track** of things like books to read, movies to see, restaurants to try, places to go? Simple ways:

- Use a notebook with divided sections to make and keep separate lists.

- Create a "Wanna" folder with lists for the things you "wanna" do.

- Use your contact management software or PDA to create electronic notes for each category.

Establish **routines** to help you get things done in a timely manner. *Examples*: Back up your computer every Friday, change bedsheets on Saturday, enter receipts in your bookkeeping system on Monday, clean out the refrigerator before going grocery shopping.

1 Make your bed every morning. It instantly neatens up your bedroom. Time how long it takes. Challenge yourself to do it under 60 seconds.

☀ File **contact information** for services under the business category, such as landscaping or accounting. This way you can still find the service contact even if you can't remember the name of the person or company.

☀ Use your Rolodex file to store odd bits of information that you may need to access while on the telephone or filling out forms: frequent-flyer numbers, driver's license and social security numbers, health insurance numbers, credit card numbers, lock combinations, passwords, and PINs.

everyday strategies

☀ Rather than save an entire brochure or flyer for one piece of information, such as a telephone number, save just the information and discard the paper.

☀ If you look up a telephone number in the phone directory, **highlight** the entry. If you look up the same number again, add it to your personal phone directory.

☀ Create a list of **frequently called numbers,** such as your pet sitter, babysitter, veterinarian, and dentist. Post it near the telephone.

❶ If you don't have time to put photographs in albums right away, schedule 15 minutes to do it by the end of the week.

If you really dislike putting photos in albums, consider taking all of your photographs with a **digital camera.** Download and store photos electronically. Just be sure to back up your computer regularly.

Consider keeping all formal portraits (baby, school, wedding, family) in a formal **family album.** Use extra prints to create gift albums.

Scrap any photos that didn't come out right. Or put them with your photo developing receipt and bring them back next time you develop film. Some developers will give you a refund on those.

❶ When a child is born, start a videotape to **record birthdays** and special events for that child.

everyday strategies

☼ **1** Have you ever forgotten your gym shoes or towel when packing your workout bag? Write a checklist and store it in a pocket of your bag. You can also create standard **packing checklists** for volunteer meetings, children's overnights, or family camping trips.

Keep your **suitcase** packed with items you need to bring along on every trip: travel-size toiletries, folding umbrella, travel hair dryer, wrinkle releaser, and other necessities.

Think about how you can

make each LIVING space

more pleasant. You'll be

less likely to mess it up.

everyday strategies

At the beginning of each season, hang clothes so that the open end of the hanger faces toward you. As you rehang items throughout the season, turn the hanger right way around. At the **end of the season,** you'll be able to see what you wore and what you didn't wear.

If getting dressed in the morning creates a mess, figure out in the evening what you're going to wear the **next day.** It will give you time to hang up and put away whatever you decided not to wear. You'll also have more time to iron an outfit or do some laundry, if necessary.

❶ Stock extras of items that you use on a regular basis, such as ink cartridges and paper towels. Determine your needs for the next 3, 6, or 12 months, and buy in bulk.

Create a **grocery shopping** form that includes all items currently in your pantry and any others you buy regularly. List like items together: fresh fruits and vegetables, dairy, frozen items, soups, and so on. Create bold headings for these categories and leave a couple of blank lines at the end of each category for write ins.

everyday strategies

❶ Don't buy something because it's on sale. Buy because you need it.

Post your shopping form. Circle or highlight each item you need to buy on your next trip to the store.

everyday strategies

☀ To minimize impulse buying, leave your credit card at home. When you shop with cash only, you tend to think twice about your purchases.

☀ Consider the **real cost** of your purchases. Think in terms of how many hours you need to work to pay for each item you want to buy. Then ask yourself if it is worth the price of your time and energy.

☀ Before purchasing something, think about where you will put it when you get it home. If you have nowhere to put it, don't buy it.

Buy clothes in coordinating shades. You'll need **fewer shoes** and accessories to go with your outfits — and you'll have more space in your closet.

Develop a wardrobe of classic styles and outfits that you can mix and match.

❶ When you buy clothing for children, keep the **child-size hanger.** It's easier for adults and children to hang small clothes on small hangers, which makes it more likely that they will get hung up.

Remember that nothing WORTH doing is easy.

everyday strategies

☀ Make a decision to purchase new items only to **replace items** that are worn-out. It will minimize clutter and save money.

☀ Go shopping only when you need something in particular. Make a list and stick to it.

☀ Keep a **running list** of items you need to buy. When you run out of an item or notice that you are running low, write it on your list. Do this with groceries, office supplies, pharmacy items. Keep your list handy so you can add to it easily.

everyday strategies

1 Aim to keep your clothes closet about half-empty. It's easier to take out and put away things when clothes are not crammed together.

Tape to the outside of drawers pictures or photographs of what goes in them so even very young **children** can keep their clothes organized.

Hang or fold matching outfits together for children who have not yet learned to coordinate colors. It will speed the process of getting dressed.

Got filing? Set your **kitchen timer** or electronic calendar for 15 minutes and start filing. When the timer goes off, stop what you are doing until next time.

Turn downtime into organizing or **catch-up time.** In 5 to 10 minutes, you can:

- balance your checkbook
- clean out your wallet
- stay on top of reading
- write a quick note
- sew a button back on

everyday strategies

1 Keep reading material and portable organizing projects with your briefcase or purse so that you can just grab and go.

1 Never leave a room without improving its appearance. Pick something up. Put it away.

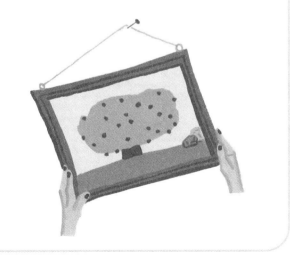

1 Question **everything** you file. *Do you really need to save the cable television statement after paying the bill? Why save paper that you will never look at again?* Shred it.

1 Designate one basket or tray as your in-box. Do not return papers to your in-box once you remove them. Move them along to the appropriate folder or to the recycling bin or wastebasket.

FINISH what you're doing before starting something new.

Use available technology to speed routine tasks:

- **Sign up for automatic bill payments.**

- **Set up an autofill program to automatically fill forms online.**

- **Program frequently called numbers into your telephone, cell phone, and fax machine.**

- **Buy postage stamps on-line.**

Take the time to learn how to put **technology** to work for you. You don't have to become a computer wiz. Just choose the features that could simplify your life and learn them one at a time.

everyday strategies

❶ Triage your mail as soon as it arrives. Toss the junk. File important things, like bills, immediately. Sort the rest into categories such as "To Read" or "To Call" or "For Bob."

❶ To prevent **paper pileup,** decide what to do with each piece of paper as it comes in: delegate, forward, file, toss, read, or respond. Set up action folders for the most common next steps.

❶ Get in the habit of developing photographs immediately upon finishing a roll. Make a note to drop them off.

Put developed photographs in albums right away.

Create a calendar file with 12 folders for the months of the year and 31 folders for the days of the month. Use it to store papers that you will need on a **future date,** such as birthday cards purchased in advance, directions to a party, or airline tickets. Store items in the appropriate day or month folder. Add "Check calendar file" to your daily to-do list to get into the habit of looking in it every day.

Buy an assortment of **greeting cards** to have on hand for unexpected events: get well, sympathy, congratulations, new baby, thank you, birthday, anniversary, blank. Store them in a hanging file folder, binder, or special card box.

❶ Schedule **filing time** at least once a week or when your "To File" folder gets full.

If you find yourself backsliding into old behaviors, be glad! If you recognize a behavior, you can change it. Recommit to your GOAL and go back to trying on the new behavior.

When bills arrive, quickly scan the inserts for any helpful or important information. Then save only the bill and the return envelope. This eliminates about half the volume of paper.

Pay bills as they come, and you won't have to set aside a chunk of time to do them all at once. Or set up **automatic bill payments.** You'll have less incoming mail to open, sort, and file. And you'll spend less time writing checks and stamping and addressing the envelopes.

everyday strategies

Reduce the volume of mail and number of checks you have to write each month. **Consolidate** bills wherever possible — long-distance, local, and cell service; home and auto insurance; and credit cards. You might even save some money.

❶ If you don't need to save utility bill statements for tax purposes, keep just the current month's statements for easy reference to customer service contacts.

everyday strategies

Consider having credit card and bank statements delivered via **e-mail** to reduce the amount of mail you get. If you do this, set up electronic folders to store statements. And be sure to back up files regularly.

- Have your bank store your canceled checks. If you need to retrieve one, you can request it.

- When you file a paper, take a **quick look** through the folder to see if there's anything in there you can toss.

Monitor your self-talk. If you think to yourself, "I'm such a slob," immediately negate that thought with "I'm getting MORE organized every day."

❶ Always put new documents in the front of a file folder so that your papers are filed in reverse chronological order.

❶ Avoid placing folders and papers directly on your **desk** unless you are physically working with them.

❶ Create new project folders immediately, to give all related paperwork a home.

❶ Put papers back in a file folder as soon as you are done with them.

everyday strategies

Use business card holders in your **purse** for storing frequent-flyer cards, frequent-buyer cards, or membership cards. Or type and print the numbers on a sheet of paper and have it reduced to fit in your wallet.

Organize ATM, debit card, credit card, and other receipts in your purse or car with a mini expandable file or coupon organizer. Schedule time to go through them daily, weekly, or monthly.

everyday strategies

Keep anything you might need on the road in your **car trunk,** and you won't have to worry about storing it anywhere else. *Examples:* maps, beach blanket, folding chair(s), first-aid kit, rain slicker.

Always fill your **gas tank** when it gets down to one-quarter or one-half full.

Balance your checking account on-line every few days. Then you can shred ATM and debit charge receipts that have been posted, instead of hanging on to them for the entire month.

Slow down. Practice the concept of "pace, not race." Walk and talk more SLOWLY. Give yourself more time to get where you're going and to complete your work.

CHAPTER 6

Clutter Control

Daily organizing is the best line of defense against clutter. Don't just put things down; put them away. And clean up as you go. Also keep in mind that clutter doesn't let itself in the door. The more trouble you have parting with things, the more careful you need to be about acquiring things. Keep in mind that unplanned purchases often end up as clutter. Make the decision not to bring something into your house, and you won't have to make a decision later about what to do with it.

Do a quick **5-minute pickup** every night before going to bed. Assign family members to each room. Hand little ones a pillowcase so they can help with nightly clutter rounds.

When you have 10 minutes free, pick up and put away 10 things that belong somewhere else.

clutter control

If you see something in a catalog that you might want to buy, tear out the page and the order form and throw out the rest. Staple the page(s) together with the order form and put them in a file labeled **"To Buy."** This makes it easier to find what you were interested in without having to save the whole catalog.

❶ Never place a larger item, like a folder, on top of a smaller thing, like a receipt; you'll spend less time looking for things.

clutter control

☀ **❶** Live by the **one in/one out rule.** For every item you bring in the front door, send one item out the back door. Apply this rule to everything from clothing to paper to household items and gifts. Decide before you purchase an item what you intend to let go of to make room for your purchase.

clutter control

① Plan to **periodically purge** your belongings. Once a year is good. Twice a year is better. Or set up a schedule of regular mini household purges. Scheduling suggestions:

January: Files

May: Storage areas

June: Winter clothing

July: Children's clothing

October: Summer clothing

November/December: Toys and household furnishings

clutter control

❶ Declare one day in the spring and fall as **"donation days."** Make a note now in your daily planner or calendar.

On self-proclaimed donation days, rummage through your home looking for things that are just taking up space in your closet, things you can donate. Box or bag them up and take them to a local charity.

❶ Decide to make an annual purge part of your **spring cleaning** ritual. Cleaning your house will be easier with less stuff in it.

clutter control

Do an inventory of your children's clothing *before* going **back-to-school shopping.** If they haven't worn something in the past 12 months, either it doesn't fit or they don't like it. Add it to the donations or hand-me-down pile and make a list of any items that need to be replaced.

❶ Designate a family donation box for collecting items throughout the year. When the box is full, take it to a local charity.

clutter control

Just before Christmas or birthdays, **ask your kids** for donations of toys, books, and clothes they no longer use or want. Help kids get into the spirit by letting them know that last year's gifts would make great gifts this year for kids who might not get any otherwise.

☀ When you redecorate your bathroom or buy new sheets for your bed, don't allow the old stuff to take up valuable space in your closets for the next five years. **Donate it now,** and let someone else share in the joy of redecorating.

clutter control

☀ Establish a house rule that all **newspapers** go into the recycling bin at the end of each day, whether they've been read or not. By tomorrow, it will be old news.

☀ Hang clothes up or put them away immediately when you take them off.

No matter how much you acquire, it's virtually impossible to have it all. There's always something newer and better being introduced. Try to be HAPPY with what you already have.

clutter control

Play clutter tag. Give a roll of stickers to the kids for tagging any item that's not where it belongs. Making family members aware of their clutter trails may make them think twice about leaving things around.

❶ Make it clear that leaving personal belongings unattended may result in their being held for ransom. If a family member wants his or her stuff back, he or she will have to do an **extra chore.** If anyone chooses not to do the chore, you know that the item isn't important enough. Give the item away without guilt.

clutter control

☀ ❶ If **family members** leave their things where they don't belong, gather them up in a large garbage bag and take it out to the garage. When they ask if you've seen a particular item you picked up, tell them it's in the garage. When they ask why, tell them you found it lying around and thought it was garbage. They should get the idea pretty fast.

☀ ❶ When it seems like you need more storage space, it's probably time to eliminate some stuff. Schedule a **decluttering session.**

clutter control

☀ Put a wastebasket in every room.

☀ Keep a litter bag in your car.

☀ If you're having a yard sale, plan to drop off whatever is left at a local charity, or schedule a pickup in advance.

Pack up toys your children have outgrown. Write today's date on the box. If your kids are looking for something you packed up, you can pull it back out. But if the kids haven't missed anything in that box in six months, donate the items.

clutter control

☀ ❶ Planning a **yard sale?** Give children an incentive to sell toys and games they no longer play with and books they don't read anymore. Let them keep whatever money they get for their stuff.

☀ ❶ If something breaks and you replace it, get rid of the broken item. It is officially garbage.

clutter control

❶ Maximize your earnings by **selling used items** while they still have value. Make a decision to sell clothing while it is still in fashion. Sell books, toys, and games while they're still in demand. Sell sporting gear before it becomes outdated. Sell your cell phone, computer, or other high-tech equipment before it becomes obsolete.

❶ Remember that all donations made on or before December 31 are tax deductible in the current tax year.

clutter control

① **To reduce virtual clutter:**

- **Delete all e-mail that requires no further action on your part.**

- **If you want to save an e-mail, create a folder for it on your hard drive.**

- **Avoid printing e-mails unless you absolutely need to have a hard copy.**

- **Periodically schedule some time to delete files.**

① When creating electronic folders, set them up the same way you would set up physical folders. Use subfolders within folders to organize files the same way you organize manila folders inside hanging folders.

Let go of the belief that

once a thing enters into

your POSSESSION,

you are its keeper

forevermore.

clutter control

Lots of well-intentioned gifts end up as clutter. Strategies:

- **Don't ever gush over a gift you don't like. Just say thanks.**

- **If a gift giver asks what you want, speak up.**

- **Spread the word that you don't need any more of whatever it is that you keep getting.**

- **Drop hints about what you would love to get.**

- **See if you can exchange a gift you don't like or can't use.**

- **Keep gifts for a set time; then donate them.**

- **Pass the gift along to someone who will appreciate it.**

clutter control

1 If a gift giver learns that you no longer have the **gift item** given to you, you can simply respond, "I did appreciate your gift, but I ended up giving it to someone who really wanted/needed it."

Talk with your family about gift-giving strategies at **holidays.** Consider having each family member draw one name to buy for. It's more likely that everyone will receive something they really want or need.

clutter control

☀ **❶** Consider limiting yourself to one or two kinds of wrapping paper and one color of ribbon and bows that will work for every occasion.

☀ **❶** If necessary, restrict kids' toys to one or two rooms, to keep the rest of the house from getting cluttered.

clutter control

☀ Consider creating one or more **clutter-free zones** in your home. Pick a room and declare it off-limits to clutter. Establish rules for that room:

- If you bring it in with you, take it out with you.

- If you take it out while you're in here, put it away before leaving.

☀ Think twice before buying souvenirs on vacation. Take photographs or keep a journal instead.

☀ Keep a handled **basket** in the family room for quick pickup and containment of clutter.

Having less means being able to ENJOY what you have more.

clutter control

Set your table for a formal dinner, to discourage household members from using it as a dumping ground for backpacks, mail, books, and everything else that comes in the door.

❶ When you finish reading a book, pass it along. Or periodically purge your **book collection,** keeping only the ones that you might want to reread or save for reference.

clutter control

❶ Help kids see the relationship between clutter and time. On an evening when the house is in order, let kids know that because there's no clutter to pick up, you have time to make popcorn or cookies or whatever they're always asking for.

❶ If you "shop until you drop," clutter is the price you pay. Next time you are shopping, make a decision to postpone all impulse purchases by 24 hours. Most of the time, you'll decide it's not worth the effort to go back for it.

If you want your children to grow up understanding that the BEST things in life aren't things, decide to stop giving them so many things.

CHAPTER 7

Home Management

There is no one right way to organize anything. So don't be afraid to experiment. If your organizing system works, then it's perfect. If your system is not working, it's time to try something different. Know that the best home organizing systems are those devised by the end users. Try to get the whole family involved. Just be aware that not everyone in your household sees the benefits of getting organized. To get your family on board, you may have to get creative with incentives.

home management

❶ Establish the household rule: Whoever makes a mess is responsible for cleaning it up — now, not later.

Make regular organizing a **family project.** Tackle one room at a time together, and use the time to catch up on what's going on at school or in your child's head.

Set up an **in-box** for each family member. Have kids put permission slips, forms, and notices in your in-box when they come home. Train them to look in their in-boxes by putting dollar bills and love notes in them.

Help children learn organization skills that will last a lifetime:

- **Get them in the habit of doing homework at a set time each day.**

- **Help them organize their school-work and homework assignments with folders and binders.**

- **Purchase a small day planner for each child for writing down assignments and due dates.**

- **Encourage kids to select their outfits for the next day and pack their backpacks before going to bed.**

❶ If kids are hard to wake up or have to get up very early, put them to bed in their school clothes.

Consolidate efforts to save time and energy:

- Shop for groceries once rather than three or four times a week.

- Iron a bunch of things at one time, rather than just one.

- Double a dinner recipe and freeze half for another night.

- Buy all the birthday and other special-occasion cards you need one month in advance.

home management

Establish a **household budget** based on actual expenses. Using your checkbook register, make a list of all expenditures by category for the past six months. Total each category and divide by six to get the average monthly expense for each.

If you spend 5 minutes cleaning the bathroom three times a week, it takes only 15 minutes total. But if you wait to do it once a week, it can take a half hour to cut through the buildup of clutter and dirt.

Designate one area in your home as a **bill-paying place,** and keep there everything you need to pay the bills, including: unpaid bills, calculator, pens, pencils, stapler, stamps, envelopes, and blank checks. Store bill-paying supplies in nearby drawers or cabinets, or put them in a portable storage bin that you can stash somewhere when not in use.

Type standard lists of instructions and directions for your **babysitter** or pet sitter so you can just print them as needed.

Recognize that when you make changes, it takes time for others to adjust to those CHANGES. If you've always been the messy one, it's possible that family members have been using your messiness as an excuse to be messy themselves.

home management

☀ Designate one drawer or basket as a temporary holding place for **stray items:** buttons, eyeglasses, single socks, and anything that appears to be homeless. If a family member is looking for something, you can say, "Did you check the basket?" Periodically, have family members claim whatever is theirs and put it away.

☀ Sometimes the best strategy for dealing with a teen's messy room is to close the door.

home management

Develop a schedule for **laundry:** Designate certain days for certain types of laundry, or if you do laundry daily, let everyone know that anything that needs to be washed should be in the laundry room by a certain time and can be picked up after such-and-such time.

home management

Laundry is quicker and easier to do when clothes are already separated into wash type. Train family members to sort their laundry into whites, lights, and darks. Use three separate baskets or a triple-compartment laundry sorter in the **laundry room.** Use a permanent marker to label each basket or compartment: whites, lights, and darks.

1 Teach your family to turn shirts, pants, and socks right side out so you don't have to do it for everyone. Establish a reward for doing it.

Put a "dirty clothes collector" in each bedroom. Ideally, this is a lightweight basket or bag that can be easily carried to the laundry room.

If more than one family member is responsible for doing laundry (or you wish other family members *would* do laundry), try this: Write or type the washing and drying instructions for each type of wash on a slip of paper and pin or tape it to the outside of each basket or compartment.

☀ If **missing socks** are a problem, have everyone pin pairs of socks together. Wash and dry them with pins still in them. Have a place in every bedroom, preferably near the dirty-clothes hamper or basket, for keeping a supply of safety pins handy.

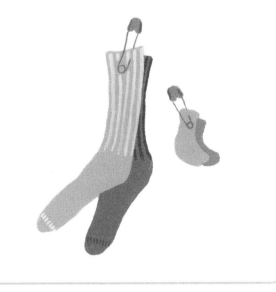

Color-code your children's clothing. Dot clothing tags and the toes of socks, using a different-colored laundry marker for each child. Then anyone can do the job of sorting and folding without having to know whose clothes are whose.

Fold or hang each item as you remove it from the **dryer.** Use the dryer top for folding and sorting; place folded clothes in the basket at your feet. Use the basket to carry clean laundry.

☀️ Don't do laundry that isn't prepared as requested.

☀️ **Premeasure** laundry detergent into zippered plastic food bags to take to the Laundromat. Use a film canister to take along 20 quarters.

Spend some time organizing your laundry room and cleaning closet. It makes chores more pleasant when you can easily reach the supplies you need without getting hit on the head with dust mops and brooms.

Simplify meal planning and shopping. Keep track of your **dinner menus** for a month. Write each complete menu on the front of an index card, and list the ingredients on the back. At the end of the month, you will have 28 dinner ideas to choose from each week. Simply add the ingredients you need to your weekly shopping list.

☀ With older children and teenagers, make it clear that privileges depend on response to family requests. If assigned chores don't get done on time, no privileges are awarded.

Experiment with precooked, ready-to-cook, and **ready-to-eat items** from the supermarket. They cost a little more, but sometimes it's worth it. *Ideas:* marinated meats for the barbecue, bagged salads, roasted chicken, and frozen stir-fry meals.

❶ If your children go grocery shopping with you, have them locate the coupon items for you. You might even offer them cash for the value of the coupons in return for helping to do the shopping, loading, and unloading the car and putting food away.

Look for Web sites that offer recipes searchable by ingredient. It's a big help when you have an abundance of a perishable item.

☀ Use a dishpan to collect all the dirty dishes from the table.

☀ Sort knives, spoons, and forks as you put them into the **dishwasher** to make it easier to put them away when they're clean.

home management

-☀- **1** Trade the chore you most hate doing with another household member's most hated chore.

-☀- **1** If there's a chore you put off doing because you hate it, time it. It may not take as long as you think, and once you realize that, it will be easier to make yourself do it.

Organizing is not a one-time-and-you're-done kind of job. It's an ONGOING process.

Do quick little cleanups often:

- **Use a no-wipe daily shower cleaning spray to prevent soap scum buildup.**

- **Wipe sink, faucets, and countertop after the final use every morning. Use a washcloth or hand towel that's headed for the laundry.**

- **Keep frequently used cleaning supplies in your bathroom and kitchen so that you can clean at your convenience.**

❶ Stagger wake-up times for better traffic control (and less fighting) in the bathroom on school days.

Tackling all the **housework** yourself is not doing your children any favors. Get your children to help with laundry, dishes, cleaning, and other chores. Offer a per-job salary or weekly allowance. Reward points as incentive. Give praise for a job well-done to help build self-esteem.

1 If you haven't already, make it a point to try revolutionary new **cleaning products** like cleaner-on-board wet mops, pre-moistened wipes, and ready-to-use toilet brush cleaners.

home management

Make a list of chores that need to be done on a regular basis. Have family members initial the chores they don't mind doing. You do the same. Each of you can then take responsibility for those chores and rotate the ones everyone dislikes.

Try the **job jar** method of assigning chores: Write regular chores on individual slips of paper and put them into a jar. Each week, have family members take turns pulling out the slips of paper.

Create a separate job jar or envelope for jobs that fall outside the weekly routine.

❶ Keep a **log book** near the phone for recording phone messages and other notes for family members. It's a handy reference if you ever need to find a phone number that's not in your personal directory.

❶ If you think of something at work that you need to do at home, leave yourself a **voice mail** message.

CHAPTER 8

Schedules & To-Do's

Organize your schedule around your priorities. The more control you exert over your schedule, the more control you will have over the direction of your life. Accept the fact that you are not likely to accomplish everything on your to-do list. It's okay. Sometimes you just need to "be" rather than be doing. The most important things will always get done. Do make a point to focus on the task at hand. Recent scientific studies prove that multitasking is not as efficient as you might think.

schedules & to-do's

- ☀ Keep the same calendar for business and personal use. Use different-colored pencils or highlighters to distinguish between work and personal commitments.

Find a calendar or **day planner** that really suits you. You'll be more inclined to use it every day.

- ☀ Keep your schedule flexible. Create a buffer zone around each activity to accommodate for the fact that things take longer than you think and to allow for unexpected delays.

schedules & to-do's

Map out your day in 15- or 30-minute increments. You can often accomplish more by using small blocks of time to focus on a particular project.

Build a little **relaxation** time into your schedule. Your body, mind, and spirit need it.

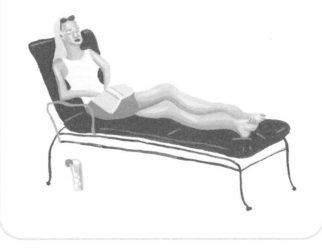

schedules & to-do's

☀ Block out one hour of time each day to work on long-range planning or goals.

☀ Block out one morning or afternoon each week for administrative tasks: filing, paying bills, ordering supplies.

☀ Schedule your most difficult tasks — those that require creative thinking and decision making — for the time of day when you have the most energy.

Schedule **routine tasks,** such as housecleaning and grocery shopping, into regular time slots on your calendar. It will help to keep your household running smoothly and ensure that you don't overbook yourself.

Do at least one thing each day that will bring you closer to a **long-term goal.** *Ideas:* Make a phone call, set up a folder, attend a meeting, set up a bank account, brainstorm an idea, ask an expert for advice.

schedules & to-do's

**Free up time by consolidating
like tasks:**

- **Check e-mail messages and return
  telephone calls once or twice a
  day, instead of all day long.**

- **Pick up and drop off dry cleaning
  at the same time.**

- **Make a list of what you need from
  the supermarket, and shop weekly
  instead of daily.**

schedules & to-do's

1 Schedule a regular time for running routine **errands,** and run them all at once.

Group errands together geographically to save time. Make a list and number stops in order.

Don't forget to schedule routine maintenance on your **car** and home to avoid costly and untimely repairs.

schedules & to-do's

☀ When you write appointments in your planner, also write in a **phone number** to call in case you're running late, want to confirm, or need to reschedule.

☀ Set your electronic calendar alarm, your watch, or an alarm clock to remind you when it is time to leave for an appointment or make an important call.

schedules & to-do's

Keep track of **family schedules** with a physician's group practice appointment book (available at office-supply stores). Multiple columns allow you to see where each family member needs to be at any given time.

❶ Schedule a family meeting once a week to review upcoming agendas.

Keep the family calendar in a central location so every family member can enter appointments and events.

If you keep doing things the same way, you're going to keep getting the same RESULTS. Accept the fact that you're going to have to change your ways.

schedules & to-do's

Create a **master list** of things to do. From this list, create your daily to-do lists.

Put the **80/20 principle** to work. Only 20 percent of the things on your to-do list are priority items. If you have 20 things on your master to-do list, identify which four (20 percent) are the most important, and focus all of your energy on getting those things done.

schedules & to-do's

Evaluate every item on your master to-do list. Move any tasks that would be nice to do, but aren't necessary, to a separate "would be nice to do" list.

❶ Decide which **one thing** on your daily to-do list is the most important thing to get done. Do that first.

End your work day by writing a to-do list for the next day.

schedules & to-do's

The secret to getting through your daily to-do list is to put fewer things on it. Just list the three most important things to do that day. If you have time left over at the end of the day, you can always add another task from your master list.

❶ Add "Unclutter my desk" to your daily to-do list until it becomes a habit.

❶ Every Monday morning or Friday night, pick a project or area to organize in the **coming week.**

schedules & to-do's

1 Schedule 15 minutes each day to work on **weekly** organizing projects. If you finish before the week is up, use the rest of the scheduled organizing time to spend with your kids, work on your novel, or do some long-range planning.

1 If you have trouble getting started each day, add to your daily to-do list a simple task, such as "Make coffee" or "Check calendar." As soon as you do it, cross it off your list and move on to the first real task of the day. A sense of accomplishment helps to get your day going in the right direction.

schedules & to-do's

Make a decision about what to do next with each piece of paper you pick up. If it's not practical to take immediate action, file the paper in an action folder. For example, if you need to reply to correspondence but must first make a phone call to obtain information, file the paper in an action folder labeled "To Call."

Go through your in-box daily.

schedules & to-do's

Keep in your **e-mail in-box** only those messages that you have yet to respond to. Delete or move other messages to subfolders within your in-box.

❶ Minimize distractions while you work. Let voice mail take messages. Close your e-mail program or lower the volume of your speakers so you can't hear incoming mail notification.

It doesn't matter where or how you start. All that matters is that you BEGIN somewhere, anywhere. START right now.

schedules & to-do's

At the beginning of each week, create time in your schedule for each one of your **priorities.** Then schedule everything else around those things.

If having more free time is a priority, schedule your free time first. Then schedule focused work time. Use the time in between for completing routine tasks.

❶ Before you take on another responsibility, ask yourself if it fits with your priorities.

1 Go on a **commitments diet.** If you are involved in activities that are not aligned with your values or priorities, consider resigning from those activities. It's okay. People will understand. Keep in mind that in stepping aside, you are giving someone else an opportunity to step forward.

Choose two or three things that you consider to be the most important to you, such as career, family, fitness, or whatever you are passionate about. Design your to-do list around these priorities.

❶ If you have trouble **saying no,** say "Can I get back to you?" You may find it easier to bow out when you don't have the pressure of giving an immediate reply.

❶ Apply the on/off rule to commitments. Before you agree to be on a committee or board, get off a committee or board.

schedules & to-do's

Delegate anything that doesn't require your knowledge and skills. Delegate to household members or hire an outside service.

Remember that in the big picture of life, your to-do list is not nearly as important as your to-be list. Schedule time to be with the people you love, in the places you love, doing the things you love to do.

❶ If it will take less than a minute to file a paper, write a check, or whatever, do it now.

schedules & to-do's

☀ Beware of the practice of leaving papers out as reminders of things to do. *Better:* Make a note of what you need to do and file the paper in a to-do folder or in a hanging file with related papers.

☀ **Simple ways to remember important things to do while you are out:**

- **Put objects that need to leave the room or house with you near the door or on the driver's seat of your car.**

- **Post a sticky note on the door-jamb.**

- **Post a sticky note on the dashboard of your car as a reminder.**

schedules & to-do's

☀ Stay on track. As you begin to do something, ask yourself why you are doing it. Is it important enough that you need to do it right now? Or can it wait until later?

☀ Make dreaded tasks more enjoyable. **Listen to music** while performing the task, or give yourself a little reward after.

schedules & to-do's

❶ Make a note in your calendar or day planner to start gathering all your **tax documentation** on or around January 15.

❶ Schedule an appointment with your tax preparer in late January/ early February.

Deliver all tax documentation to your tax preparer no later than February 15, or use that as your start date if you are preparing your own taxes.

schedules & to-do's

At the end of the year, transfer special dates to remember to your new calendar.

☀ Make a note in your calendar to do a back-to-school clothing inventory in July and a toy purge in December. (See related tips in chapter 6: Clutter Control.)

schedules & to-do's

Note birthdays, anniversaries, and special dates in your electronic calendar, in your day planner, or on a wall calendar. Also, pencil in reminders for routine automobile maintenance (inspections, oil changes, tire rotation) and for routine home maintenance (change air conditioning and heating filters and check smoke detectors).

① **Plan ahead** as much as possible to save time, money, frustration, hassles, and disappointments later. *Example:* If you know you have a week off in July, start making vacation plans in January or February.

Don't OVERWHELM yourself by thinking about all the work you have to do. Just do what you can do today.

schedules & to-do's

❶ Never forget a special occasion again. Sign up for a free or fee-based e-mail reminder on the Internet.

Schedule time in late December/early January to go through all the files in your filing cabinet. Toss or shred any papers you no longer need to save. Consolidate or add file folders as necessary. Use a binder clip to mark the file where you left off, if you need to finish the project another day.

index